# RN SUBM

**CDR David Hobbs MBE RN Retd**

# INTRODUCTION

The first practical submarine design was the work of John P Holland, an Irish emigrant to the United States; the Admiralty purchased the rights to his design early in the twentieth century and ordered its first boats from Vickers under an exclusive contract. Evolution followed rapidly through the 'A', 'B' and 'C' classes to the 'D' class which introduced side ballast tanks, diesel engines, bow torpedo tubes disposed vertically. All subsequent conventional designs could be said to be improvements on the later 'E' class which formed the 'backbone' of the Submarine Service during the 1914-18 war.

The 'H' class had the reputation of being the fastest divers in the Service but the much larger 'J' and 'K' classes represented an attempt to produce large, ocean-going boats capable of high speed on the surface that would allow them to work with the battle-fleet. The latter were steam-powered with a speed on the surface of 24 knots. The 'L' class marked a return to diesel-electric propulsion and more modest dimensions; they were considered to be the best all-round boats of their generation but the 'M' class represented an attempt to build submarine monitors that was not successful. M-1 was lost in 1925 and the big guns removed from the other two. M-2 was converted to carry and operate a seaplane but was lost in 1932 and M-3 was transformed into a submarine minelayer. The 'R' boats represented the first attempt to produce a submarine hunter/killer design and their underwater speed of 15 knots was not equalled until after 1945. During the First World War 54 British submarines were lost in operations.

The bulk of British submarine construction was shared between only four yards; Chatham Dockyard, Vickers, Cammell Laird and Scotts. This made increased production difficult during the period of re-armament from the late 1930s and some work was spread to Vickers' Walker Yard, Devonport and Portsmouth Dockyards. Three types were in production in 1939; the larger 'T' class, the medium 'S' class and the smaller 'U' class which all proved successful in service. The 'A' class was developed during the war for Pacific operations and had a higher surface speed and greater radius of action than the 'T's. 77 British submarines were lost during the 1939-45 war.

After 1945 the Royal Navy initially relied on modernised boats of wartime design before building the very successful 'Porpoise' and 'Oberon' classes. Nuclear-powered submarines first appeared fifty years ago with the prototype 'Dreadnought' launched in 1960. She was followed by the 'Valiant', Swiftsure', 'Trafalgar' and 'Astute' classes built in sequence, interspersed with the 'Resolution' and 'Vanguard' class nuclear-powered ballistic missile submarines armed with Polaris and Trident missiles respectively. The last British conventional submarines, the 'U' class were withdrawn from service prematurely in the mid 1990s and sold to Canada. In 2011 Britain has a small force of capable nuclear-powered submarines which draw on the rich history of innovative design and construction illustrated in the following pages.

David Hobbs
Crail, 2011

The first British submarines were built by Vickers at Barrow-in-Furness, at a cost of £35,000 each, to a design by the brilliant Irish-American inventor John Philip Holland. They were given numbers rather than names but were usually referred to as 'Holland-boats'. Here HM Submarine Number 3 is passing HMS VICTORY, often used in the background of early twentieth century warship photographs to show the radical advances being made in technology. The bearded petty officer seated on the hatch is the coxswain steering the boat with the external wheel. The tall mast supported by a wire stay is the periscope.

*(Syd Goodman Collection)*

Three Holland boats in the upper reaches of Portsmouth harbour in 1904 secured alongside the submarine support ship HMS HAZARD. She was a former torpedo gunboat built in 1894 which had been moored in Barrow while the first boats were built under the command of Captain Reginald Bacon RN, the first Inspecting Captain of Submarines. She left Barrow with her submarines in 1902 for Portsmouth and used them to evaluate submarine capability and to train surface ships in anti-submarine tactics. Their small 45 hp petrol engine gave them a maximum speed of 8 knots on the surface and an electric motor drove them at up to 5 knots submerged for short periods. An hour was the longest practical period the boats could stay dived.

*(Syd Goodman Collection)*

HM Submarine Number 1 was sold to T W Ward as scrap for £410 but foundered near the Eddystone Lighthouse on 5 November 1913 while under tow to the breaker's yard. She was located by the mine-hunter HMS BOSSINGTON on 14 April 1981 and subsequently raised for restoration and display in the RN Submarine Museum at Gosport. She is seen here in Number 12 Dock in Devonport Dockyard on 1 December 1982 prior to restoration. Holland boats were built for the American, British and several foreign navies but Number 1 is the only example known to have survived. (*Ben Warlow Collection*)

The Admiralty signed an exclusive contract with Vickers for the design and construction of submarines and 13 slightly larger 'A' class boats followed the Hollands. They had an operational capability and were optimised for coastal defence against enemy raiders. About 40 feet longer than the earlier boats, they cost £41,000 each and the prominent markings on the conning tower are an example of one of the early methods used to identify boats on the surface. No scheme was particularly successful and they were frequently changed prior to 1914.

*(Ben Warlow Collection)*

HM Submarine A-13 piping a ship to starboard as she passes HMS VICTORY in Portsmouth harbour. Identification of surfaced boats had resolved itself by this stage into painting the pennant number as conspicuously as possible on a vertical surface. Early submarines had no room for a signals rating onboard and commanding officers had to send and receive their own semaphore and light signals. The requirement to learn these and other 'trades' led to the Submarine Branch becoming known to its officers as 'The Trade'. Surface ships were instructed to pass signals to submarines slowly and patiently at this time.

*(Syd Goodman Collection)*

The eleven 'B' class boats were a further step forward with a submerged displacement of 316 tons. Apart from advancing the science of submarine warfare the new boats were given a variety of unusual tasks; B-1 for instance, was secured alongside HMS VICTORY to provide it with electrical power on Trafalgar Day 1905.

*(Ben Warlow Collection)*

HM Submarine B-4 at sea. The 'B' class were fitted with a 16-cylinder Vickers petrol engine which developed 600 hp and gave up to 12 knots on the surface in calm conditions. The 290 hp electric motor gave underwater speeds of up to 6 knots in short bursts. There were two torpedo tubes in the bow, each with a reload giving a total of 4 torpedoes. B-11 entered the Dardanelles on 13 December 1914 and torpedoed the Turkish battleship MESUDIYEH. Her commanding officer Lieutenant Norman Holbrook was awarded the VC for the exploit.

*(Syd Goodman Collection)*

The 'C' class were the last British submarines to be fitted with petrol engines. Thirty-eight were built between 1905 and 1910, most of them by Vickers but five were built by Chatham Dockyard to ensure that the Royal Dockyards understood the latest technology. The design was basically sound but the reserve of buoyancy was only 10% over their surface displacement, limiting their surfaced performance. They had a range of 1,150 miles at 8 knots. C-34, one of the Chatham-built boats, is seen here approaching the submarine base HMS DOLPHIN at Gosport.

(*Ben Warlow Collection*)

HM Submarine C-3 was the first of the 'C' class to commission in 1906. By 1918, however, she was obsolescent and was packed with explosives to ram into and destroy the viaduct that connected the Mole at Zeebrugge to the shore during the historic blocking raid on 23 April 1918.

*(Ben Warlow Collection)*

HM Submarine C-38, the last of the 'C' class to be completed, leaving Portsmouth with the Round Tower and cathedral in the background. Ten 'C's were lost in the First World War and the remainder scrapped soon after the end of hostilities with the exception of C-4 which was used for trials until 1922.

(*Syd Goodman Collection*)

The 'D' class represented a major step forward in British submarine design. They were the first boats to have diesel engines and the first to have radio transmitters, previous boats only had receivers. Displacement increased to 620 tons dived and the class was intended for longer ranged operations beyond coastal waters. The RN regarded them as such an advance that D-1 was built at Barrow under conditions of great secrecy behind screens. Four were lost in World War 1 patrolling the North Sea and Heligoland Bight. D-8, seen here, paid off for disposal in July 1919. *(Ben Warlow Collection)*

HM Submarine D-8 entering Portsmouth. Among the many innovations introduced in the 'D' class, they were the first British boats to be designed with external ballast tanks. Ten were originally ordered but the last two, D-9 and D-10 were modified into the first two units of the 'E' class, E-1 and E-2, while building.

(*Ben Warlow Collection*)

In 1912 a committee of RN submarine officers recommended the construction of a large, fast 'overseas' type of submarine displacing over 1,000 tons and capable of 20 knots on the surface. NAUTILUS was built to a Vickers' design to meet the requirement but given low priority after the outbreak of war in 1914. She was eventually completed at a cost of £203,850 in 1917 with a dived displacement of 1,441 tons and capable of 17 knots on the surface. Her diesel engines were a new Vickers' design which proved to be unreliable and, outdated by wartime progress, she never entered operational service. She is seen here at Barrow-in-Furness shortly after completion. In 1918 she became a battery-charging vessel and in 1922 she was sold for scrap.

*(Syd Goodman Collection)*

The 'D's had been generally well-liked but technology was advancing so rapidly that six boats of an improved 'E' class were ordered from Vickers under the 1910-11 Estimates. After the outbreak of World War 1 further orders for 50 more 'E's were placed with Vickers and 12 other builders. Chatham Dockyard produced a simplified version in E-12 which was adopted as the standard for all subsequent boats. Unit cost rose to £101,900 for the first six. E-4, seen here with two deck guns, was completed with beam as well as bow 18-inch torpedo tubes but the former were deleted in later boats.

*(Ben Warlow Collection)*

Two 'E' class boats were built for the Royal Australian Navy, AE-1 and AE-2. AE-1 commissioned at Portsmouth on 28 February 1914 and arrived in Sydney 83 days later. In September 1914 she took part in Australian operations to occupy a number of German territories including Bougainville and New Guinea. On 14 September she failed to return from a patrol off Rabaul. Searches failed to find any trace of either the boat or any survivors and it was presumed that she sank while carrying out a practice dive, perhaps after striking an uncharted pinnacle of rock. Her wreck has never been located.

*(Ben Warlow Collection)*

HM Submarine E-23 and other 'E' class boats alongside a depot ship. The 'E's were the first British boats in which the hull was divided into watertight compartments; two bulkheads creating three sections although the boat could not remain afloat if either of the largest two compartments was completely flooded. The bulkheads did strengthen the hull, however, allowing a greater diving depth to be achieved. They were also the first to have a flushing toilet, operated by a complicated sequence of valves, which could be used while dived. Note the 4-inch gun partially enclosed in the casing when not cleared for action.

*(Syd Goodman Collection)*

HM Submarine E-11 penetrated the Dardanelles into the Sea of Marmara in 1915, commanded by Lieutenant Commander N M Nasmith RN who was awarded the VC for his exploits. He sank the Turkish battleship HARRIDIN BARBAROSSA with a torpedo and made a raft out of captured Turkish ships that allowed D'Oyley Hughes, his First Lieutenant, to swim ashore and blow up a railway viaduct over which trains had been taking enemy troops to Gallipoli. Note the camouflaged casing intended to make the boat more difficult to spot from the air while it was at periscope depth.    (*Ben Warlow Collection*)

The 'G' class introduced a double-hull design which gave a much greater reserve of buoyancy, 45-50%, which improved performance on the surface. The greater buoyancy, however, meant bigger ballast tanks were needed which were slower to fill than those in the 'E's and, thus, diving took longer. They were also slow to drain leading to stability problems on surfacing. G-4 and G-10 are seen here alongside the depot-ship HMS TITANIA.

*(Syd Goodman Collection)*

The 'J' class were produced at the instigation of Admiral Jellicoe, C-in-C Grand Fleet who believed that the Germans had submarines with a surface speed of 22 knots, capable of operating with the High Seas Fleet and wanted something similar. The hull form developed by the Director of Naval Construction's Department remains, even today, the best ever tested for its speed/length ratio but it was still only capable of 19½ knots. One was a war-loss and the remaining 5 of the class were donated to Australia at the end of hostilities. J-5 is seen here off Plymouth Hoe with Smeaton's Tower and the Citadel in the background. She was eventually scuttled in the Bass Strait after several years in reserve during the 1920s.

*(Syd Goodman Collection)*

HM Submarine J-7 was ordered from the outset by the Royal Australian Navy and built by Devonport Dockyard incorporating several changes from the basic 'J' class design. Like the others she had three diesel motors producing a total of 3,600 hp on three shafts, with two electric motors developing a total of 1,350 hp on the wing shafts. 17 knots proved a realistic sea speed but she was theoretically capable of 19½. Like the rest of her class, she was too slow for work with the surface fleet but too fast, big and expensive for routine patrol work. She was eventually sunk with J-3 as a breakwater inside Port Phillip Bay in Melbourne where their remains can still be seen.

*(Syd Goodman Collection)*

HM Submarine V-3 was one of four 'V' class boats designed by Vickers to meet a 1912 RN requirement for small 'coastal' submarines. She had a dived displacement of 486 tons and cost £75,799. She is seen here at Barrow-in-Furness in 1916. The 'V's had two 18-inch torpedo tubes in the bow and a ship's company of eighteen. Two diesel engines developed a total of 900hp giving a speed of 14 knots on the surface and an electric motor of 380hp gave 9 knots dived. Whilst they were satisfactory, wartime operations revealed little need for such small boats and all four were soon discarded at the end of hostilities.

*(Syd Goodman Collection)*

The 'W' class comprised four small, coastal boats of 508 tons submerged displacement built under licence by Armstrong to a Schneider-Laubeuf design. Speed was 13 knots on the surface and 8½ knots dived; complement was nineteen. As with the 'V' class, wartime experience showed little need for these boats and manning them with scarce RN submarine crews was thought to be a waste of time. In consequence, all four were sold to the Italian Navy, which needed small boats for operations in the Aegean Sea, soon after their completion in 1916.

(*Ben Warlow Collection*)

The design of the 'L' class began as an improved 'E' and L-1 and L-2 were actually begun as E-57 and E-58. They had four 21-inch bow torpedo tubes and a 4-inch gun was mounted at bridge level with its own access trunk. Submerged displacement exceeded 1,000 tons for the first time reaching 1,074 in the first 8 boats and 1,150 in the later groups. L-21 is seen here in the lighter paint scheme used by the Mediterranean Fleet in November 1927. *(Syd Goodman Collection)*

HM Submarine L-71 was built by Scott's and completed in 1919, just too late for war service. The designers had hoped that the third batch of the 'L' class would achieve 17 knots on the surface but, disappointingly, they only achieved 12½. L-71 was modified with a more streamlined conning tower to improve underwater speed and modified propellers which enabled her to reach 14 knots on the surface. She was sold for scrap in 1938. All three groups of the 'L' class had a maximum diving depth of 250 feet although one boat, L-2, was recorded as having dived to below 300 feet in 1918 when attacked by USN destroyers which mistook her for a U-boat.

(*David John Weller*)

HM Submarines L-1 to L-9 were ordered in August 1916; a further batch L-10 to L-35, excepting L-13 which was deemed to be unlucky, were ordered in December 1916. A third batch commencing with L-50 was ordered in 1917 but boats that were incomplete were cancelled and broken up after the armistice. L-19, one of the second batch is seen entering harbour in Malta flying a paying-off pennant while serving with the Mediterranean Fleet in 1929. (*T. Ferrers-Walker Collection*)

HM Submarine L-25 about to enter harbour on 29 July 1929. The men on the casing are taking wires and fenders from their stowages in the casing and the man bending is taking the kinks out of a heaving-line by trailing it in the sea and coiling it carefully into his left hand. The 4-inch gun has been removed to allow expansion of the bridge structure.

(*Syd Goodman Collection*)

HM Submarines L-18, L-21, L-23 and L-26 alongside the depot-ship HMS LUCIA at Gibraltar during Home Fleet exercises in January 1933. The battleships RODNEY and NELSON are visible beyond them. All four boats have retained their 4-inch guns and L-26 has hers trained slightly to starboard for maintenance showing how the streamlined fairing rotated with it. The second batch of 'L' class boats had four bow tubes with eight torpedoes; the third batch six tubes and twelve torpedoes and a second 4-inch gun on the after part of the bridge deck.

(*Ken Kelly Collection*)

HM Submarine L-69 was one of the third, or L-50, batch of the successful 'L' class which represented the last evolution of the design. They had six 21-inch torpedo-tubes in the bow and a submerged displacement of 1,150 tons. Seventeen boats of this batch were cancelled when the First World War ended but eight were sufficiently advanced to merit completion. L-69 was completed by Rosyth Dockyard in 1923 as the last boat of the class. She was sold for scrap in 1939.

*(David John Weller)*

Some of the 'L' class continued to serve into the Second World War. L-27 torpedoed a 7,000 ton German merchant ship off Cherbourg on 15 October 1940 but was then rammed by one of its escorts. She is seen here with her damaged conning tower alongside Fort Blockhouse. This was to be the only torpedo success by an 'L' boat during the war.

*(Syd Goodman Collection)*

Not quite what it seems. This publicity photograph was distributed by the Admiralty and the original caption read "*War scene reconstructed for a film; a British submarine disguised as a German U-boat. Lieutenant Commander Auten VC is the adviser on naval detail*". Unfortunately it did not mention the real identity of the boat or the name of the film.

(*Steve Bush Collection*)

HM Submarine S-1 was an experimental steam-driven submarine ordered from Vickers in 1913, intended to demonstrate high surface speed and long range. The small funnel was folded down electrically and then sealed to prevent water ingress, a process that took 11 minutes. Shutting down the boilers caused a considerable increase in heat inside the boat and trials were not altogether successful. The unusual arrangement of the bow torpedo tubes can be seen in this photograph taken in dry dock. In 1917 she was converted into a surface escort and renamed SWORDFISH.
(*Ben Warlow Collection*)

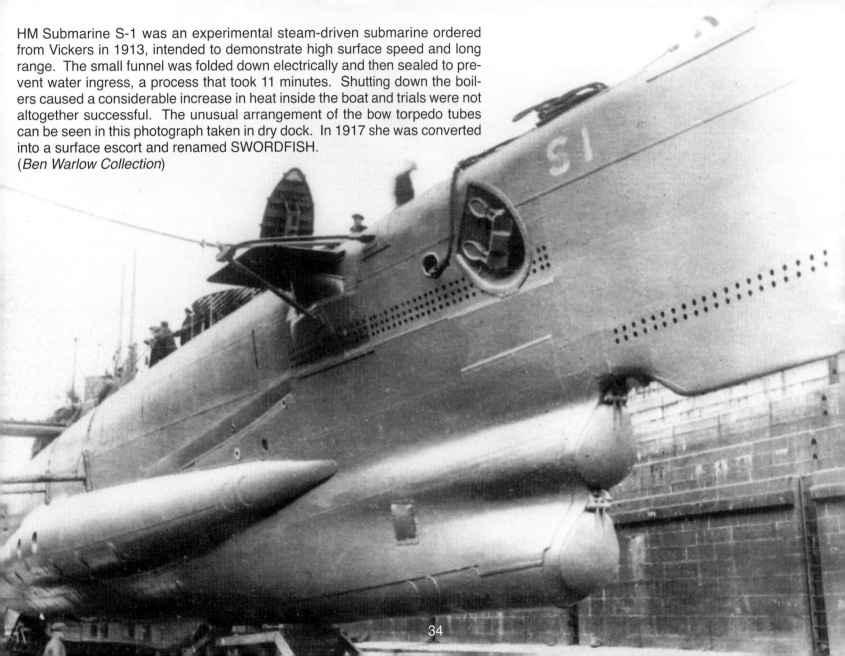

The 'K' class boats were among the most unusual submarines to serve in the Royal Navy and were, in some ways, ahead of their time. They followed S-1 and the 'J' class in an attempt to create a submarine that had a surface speed high enough to operate with the Grand Fleet and used steam turbines of 10,500 hp to achieve 24 knots. K-3, the first boat to complete, is seen here at high speed on the surface. 17 'K's were built to the basic design, 6 of which were lost in accidents, most of them after 1918. Their considerable size resulted in depth-keeping and control problems made worse by a maximum diving depth of only 200 feet. They were 330 feet long which meant that at a steep diving angle, the bow could easily dip below the maximum permissible depth while the stern was just below the surface. *(Ben Warlow Collection)*

HM Submarine K-26 was the only unit of a second batch of 'K's to be completed and was finished without urgency in 1923. Many of the faults in the earlier batch were ironed out but she cost £340,000 and had a dived displacement of 2,566 tons. The 'K's tended to be bow-heavy at speed on the surface and the flared structure, seen to advantage here, was fitted to cure the problem; it was known as a 'swan bow' to her ship's company. K-26 survived in service until 1931 when she was withdrawn and scrapped because her displacement exceeded the limit set by the London Naval Treaty.

*(T. Ferrers-Walker Collection)*

Four 'M' class submarines were ordered from Vickers in 1916 in place of the last 4 'K' boats which were cancelled. The 'M's were large boats of 1,946 tons submerged displacement intended to use gunfire rather than expensive torpedoes to sink enemy shipping and for coastal bombardment work. The gun, seen here forward of the bridge on M-3 was a 12-inch Mark IX L/40 originally used in Formidable class battleships. It was fired from a shallow dived position with the end of the barrel just clear of the surface at a range of about 1,300 yards, sighted through the periscope. The boat had to surface to reload, the procedure taking about 3 minutes. She also had four 21-inch torpedo tubes. (*Syd Goodman Collection*)

HM Submarine M-2 was converted to operate a Parnall Peto seaplane in 1925 and had a hangar, handling crane and cata-pult forward of the conning tower. Pilot and observer both qualified for flying and submarine specialist pay. The technique of launching the aircraft involved opening the hangar door as soon as the superstructure broke surface, even though the stern ballast tanks were not yet pumped empty, holding the boat on the surface with forward speed on the hydroplanes. M-2 was lost on 26 January 1933, probably because the hydroplanes failed, causing the stern to drop and drag the hangar below the surface, causing the boat to fill rapidly with water and dive to the bottom. Witnesses certainly saw her go under stern first.

*(Syd Goodman Collection)*

HM Submarine M-3 was converted into a submarine minelayer in 1927 in order to evaluate the equipment intended for the projected Porpoise class. She carried 100 mines on a conveyor belt fitted on top of the pressure hull, enclosed within the enlarged casing. The mines were ejected through a door at the stern. She is seen here sailing from Portsmouth during the trials programme which was completed in 1932, after which she saw no further service and was broken up.

(*National Museum of the Royal Navy*)

The 12 'R' class submarines were ordered from a variety of builders and dockyards in December 1917 and were the first to be designed specifically to attack other submarines; the precursors of the modern hunter/killer type. The streamlined hull had a refined shape tapering to a single screw aft. They were capable of reaching 15 knots whilst dived, a speed that would not be matched for another 25 years; surface speed was only 9 knots. The Admiralty thought that ASDIC had removed much of the threat from hostile submarines but failed to see how good the 'R' boats were and scrapped most in 1923. They kept R-10, seen here in Plymouth Sound during 1927, together with R-4 for anti-submarine warfare training. They had one 240 hp diesel and one 1,200 hp electric motor. Armament was six 18-inch torpedo tubes with twelve torpedoes. R-10 was sold for scrap in 1929.

*(T. Ferrers-Walker Collection)*

HM Submarine X-1 was built at Chatham Dockyard, laid down in November 1921, completed in June 1923 and is seen here in 1927. She was then the largest boat built for the Royal Navy at 3,600 tons dived displacement and was intended to act as a long-range commerce raider. Two diesel engines developed a total of 7,000 hp giving her a speed on the surface of just over 19 knots and she had an endurance of 21,500 miles at 8 knots which was greater than that of most cruisers at the time. Her armament of four 5-inch guns in two twin mounts was intended to allow her to dispatch merchant ships quickly and engage warships up to destroyer size.

(*T. Ferrers-Walker Collection*)

X-1 in March 1931. She was found to be too slow and not agile enough to fight a destroyer with any great chance of success on the surface and would be better off using her six torpedo tubes which negated much of the design's purpose and no repeats were built. The range-finder on the bridge was too low and she was not a steady gun platform. She was placed into reserve in 1933, deleted from service in 1936 and scrapped in 1937; the only British submarine to be both laid down and broken up between 1918 and 1939.

*(T. Ferrers-Walker Collection)*

The destroyer depot ship HMS VULCAN with H-32, H-47, H-49, H-50 and the training boat R-4 alongside. The 'H' class had a complicated origin stemming from Admiralty fears that British boats were not being built fast enough. Charles M Schwabb of the Bethlehem Steel Company offered to build 20 boats for Britain in 5½ months at $500,000 (£125,000 at the time) each in December 1914 but President Wilson objected that this breached US neutrality laws. To get round them, the first 10 boats were assembled from kits by Canadian Vickers in Montreal but at increased time and cost. In 1917 the Admiralty contracted Vickers to build 12 boats to an improved 'H' design and then a further batch from a variety of yards but most of these were cancelled after the Armistice.

*(Syd Goodman Collection)*

H-23, H-34 and a third, unidentified, boat carrying out 'officer-of-the-watch' manoeuvres. Twenty-two British-built boats of this class were completed, some of which remained in service into the Second World War. They were well-liked by their crews and were the first British boats to have a 'battery tank' remote from the conning tower. This greatly reduced the chance of seawater entering the battery and generating chlorine gas.

(*Syd Goodman Collection*)

The last British-built 'H's had British replicas of the original American machinery and were slightly longer then the first batch. Submerged displacement rose from 434 to 503 tons. Of interest, they were unstable when the batteries were removed for maintenance and changing them alongside a depot ship required careful ballasting. H-33 is seen underway with the battleship IRON DUKE in the background. (*National Museum of the Royal Navy*)

From the late 1920s British submarines began to be given names rather numbers. HMS SEAL was one of 6 Porpoise class minelaying submarines which used the equipment developed in M-3 but which only carried 50 mines. She was built in Chatham Dockyard, the last of the class, and launched in 1938. She was laying mines in the Kattegat on 5 May 1940 when she was seriously damaged and forced to surface by a mine, perhaps one of her own. Many submariners believed the superstition that a minefield's first victim would be the boat that laid it. SEAL attempted to reach Swedish territorial waters off Goteborg but was captured by 2 Arado seaplanes and then towed into a German port. The German Navy repaired her and operated her as U-B until scuttling her on 3 May 1945. She was subsequently raised and scrapped.

(*National Museum of the Royal Navy*)

The 'O' class were designed for long-range patrol duties and had an endurance of 11,400 miles at 8 knots which made them suitable for operations in the Pacific. The lead-boat OBERON was built in Chatham Dockyard, launched in 1926 and was followed by 2 similar boats, OTWAY and OXLEY, built by Vickers for the Royal Australian Navy. This first group, by then all in service with the Royal Navy, are seen here Mediterranean-moored on a port visit. OBERON and OTWAY survived the Second World War and were scrapped in 1945 at Rosyth and Inverkeithing respectively. OXLEY was torpedoed in error by TRITON on 10 September 1939 off Norway and lost with 4 officers and 49 men, her whole ship's company.

*(Fulvio Petronio)*

HM Submarine OSIRIS, seen here on 24 May 1930, was one of the second batch of 6 'O' boats; she was built by Vickers and launched in 1928. The class introduced a number of significant improvements including a diving depth of 500 feet and power-loading for the eight 21-inch torpedo tubes. Underwater speed failed to reach the designed 9 knots, however, because too many external fittings were rough or badly fixed, faults discovered during trials with OLYMPUS. Four of the 6 later 'O's were lost in the Second World War. OSIRIS served in the Mediterranean for much of the war and then became a training boat in the East Indies Fleet at Trincomalee in 1945. She was scrapped at Durban in 1946. (*Syd Goodman Collection*)

Built by Vickers at Barrow-in-Furness and completed in 1927, HMAS OXLEY was commissioned into the Royal Australian Navy on 1 April 1927. She left the UK for a short period of operations based in Malta in February 1928 and eventually arrived in Sydney, New South Wales on 14 February 1929. Her time with the RAN was short; she paid off into reserve in 1930 and was subsequently donated to the RN, commissioning with an RN crew in April 1931 after which she sailed for Malta. On 10 September 1939 she failed to respond to a recognition challenge made by the British submarine TRITON which then torpedoed and sank her. The subsequent Board of Enquiry found that OXLEY was not in its briefed patrol area and that TRITON was not to blame.

(*David John Weller*)

The six 'O' boats were followed by classes of six similar boats beginning with the letter 'P' and four beginning with 'R'. HM Submarine ROVER is seen here arriving at Portsmouth shortly after her completion on 5 August 1931. The 'O's and 'P's had riveted external fuel tanks which tended to leak and leave a trail of oil on the surface; the 'R's cured this defect by having welded tanks. Armament comprised six bow and two stern 21-inch torpedo tubes and dived displacement was 2,030 tons. ROVER was adopted by the citizens of Winchester in December 1941 during National Savings' Warship Week. She started a refit in Singapore Dockyard in August 1941 but in February 1942, shortly before Singapore fell, she was towed to Tanjong Priok in the Dutch East Indies and then to Bombay where the refit was eventually completed. In January 1945 she joined the East Indies Fleet at Trincomalee for training but was scrapped in Durban from July 1946. (*Syd Goodman Collection*)

The 'P' class proved to be a successful design with a maximum diving depth increased to 500 feet. The tall, telescopic masts that stand out in this photograph were the visible element of the boats' low-frequency radio receiver. It proved successful in service and in one early trial, signals from Rugby Broadcast on the 1500 metre band were received by a boat dived at 50 feet in the Pacific off Japan. Another technological advance in this class was an active/passive ASDIC set which proved able to detect targets at greater ranges than previous submarine sonars. (*National Museum of the Royal Navy*)

HM Submarine POSEIDON was built by Vickers at Barrow-in-Furness and completed in 1929. She served on the China Station where she sank on 9 June 1931 after a collision with the SS YUTA twenty-one miles north of the Fleet's summer base at Wei-Hei-Wei on the north coast of China. She came to rest on the sea bed in 130 feet of water with twenty-four men on board. Eight of them were trapped in the forward compartment and of these, six managed to escape to the surface using the Davis Submarine Escape Apparatus (DSEA) operationally for the first time. Petty Officer P W Willis, the Torpedo Gunner's Mate, was awarded the Albert Medal for his part in organising the escape. (*T. Ferrers-Walker Collection*)

HM Submarine RAINBOW seen on 15 February 1932. Like her sister 'R' boats she was in the 4th Submarine Flotilla on the China Station in 1939 but moved to the Mediterranean in 1940. On 19 October 1940 she was torpedoed by the Italian submarine ENRICO TOTI while on patrol in the Strait of Otranto and sunk. (*Syd Goodman Collection*)

Exercises with the steam-powered K-26 after 1918 led the Admiralty to believe that there was still a requirement for fast submarines to operate with the battle fleet and the Thames class was designed to meet it. Turbo-charged diesels of 10,000 hp and advanced hull design gave a surface speed of just over 22 knots, barely a knot less than K-26. Twenty boats of this class were planned but their high cost at £500,000 each; the restrictions imposed by the London Naval treaty and the realisation that the next generation of battleships would be capable of 28 knots or more led to the class being limited to 3 boats, all built by Vickers. This is CLYDE in May 1937, three years after her launch. She gave good service in the Second World War, torpedoing and damaging the German battle-cruiser GNEISENAU off Trondheim on 21 June 1940 and ferrying essential supplies to beleaguered Malta from Gibraltar in 1942. In 1944 she joined the Eastern Fleet based at Trincomalee and landed SOE agents in the Andaman Islands. In all she carried out 36 war patrols before reducing to reserve at Durban in August 1945. She was scrapped there a year later.

*(Syd Goodman Collection)*

HM Submarine SEVERN was built by Vickers and completed in 1934. She served throughout the Second World War, initially at Freetown in Sierra Leone and then with the Home Fleet. In 1941 she deployed to the Mediterranean where she torpedoed and sank the Italian submarine MICHELE BIANCHI. In July 1943 she was one of a number of British boats that supported Operation 'Husky', the Allied invasion of Sicily and in 1944 deployed to the Far East and operated against the Japanese. When the war ended she was deemed to be too old and worn out to bring back to the UK and she was paid off and broken up for scrap in Bombay in 1946.

(*David John Weller*)

The first batch of what was to be the numerically large 'S' class comprised four boats built at Chatham Dockyard. STUR-GEON, seen here in May 1933 and SWORDFISH were ordered under the 1929 Estimates and intended to begin the replacement of the 'L' and 'H' classes. They were intended for operations in shallow and confined waters such as the Baltic. They had a dived displacement of 927 tons; a surface speed of 15 knots; underwater speed 10 knots and an endurance of 5,750 miles at 8 knots. STURGEON had its 3-inch gun on a disappearing mounting inside a fairing but this proved an unnecessary refinement that was not fitted to later boats. She was transferred to the Royal Netherlands Navy in 1943, renamed ZEEHOND and eventually broken up at Granton in 1947.

(*Syd Goodman Collection*)

HM Submarine SWORDFISH was launched in November 1931. The early 'S' boats suffered because too much was attempted on their design size and they inevitably 'grew' whilst building, making their stability insufficient. Also, the bridge casing drained too slowly on surfacing, trapping water high up and causing a list of up to 20 degrees; surfacing in a rough beam sea was not recommended. This defect was cured by cutting extra drain holes in the bridge structure. She failed to return from a war patrol, lost to an unknown cause off Ushant on 16 November 1940. (*Syd Goodman Collection*)

HM Submarine STARFISH was built in Chatham Dockyard as one of the first group of the 'S' class and completed in 1933. She is seen in this photograph listed to starboard so that, the original caption states, the port side can be cleaned in preparation for the 1935 Fleet Review. The seaplane carrier HMS PEGASUS, formerly ARK ROYAL the first British warship built to operate aircraft, is visible in the distance behind her. STARFISH was lost on 9 January 1940 in the Heligoland Bight after a depth-charge attack by the German minesweeper M-7.

(*David John Weller*)

HM Submarine SEAHORSE passing the 'Still & West Country' public house and the Round Tower leaving Portsmouth on 11 October 1933. The riveted hull and distinctive 'turned-up' stern are clearly visible. Note the marking to indicate a hand-wheel inside the opening in the casing and the signal rating sending a semaphore message on the bridge. She was depth-charged and sunk by vessels of the German 1st Minesweeping Flotilla in the Heligoland Bight on 7 January 1940.

(*National Museum of the Royal Navy*)

HM Submarine STERLET was one of the last 8 boats of the first 'S' class group. She is seen here being launched from Chatham Dockyard on 22 September 1937. Like her sisters she had two shafts with diesel engines delivering 1,550 hp and electric motors giving 1,440 hp. Stability was improved in these boats by an increase to 960 tons dived displacement and other small improvements making them into a most successful class. On 15 April 1940 STERLET sank the German gunnery training ship BRUMMER which was escorting a convoy from Germany to Norway. She was depth-charged by the German anti-submarine escorts UJ-125, UJ-126 and UJ-128 in the East Skagerrack on 18 April 1940 and sunk.

(*Syd Goodman Collection*)

HM Submarine SNAPPER was another of the 'S' class' first group, built by Chatham Dockyard and completed in 1934. She saw action during the Norwegian Campaign during 1940 but was sunk south of Ushant on 11 February 1941 by fifty-six depth-charges dropped from three German minesweepers, M-2, M-13 and M-25. She was the first of twelve British boats to be sunk in 1941.

(*David John Weller*)

HM Submarine SAFARI was the lead ship of the second group of 'S' boats. She was built by Cammell Laird and launched on 18 November 1941. In the Mediterranean she sank 14 Axis transport ships carrying stores to North Africa while serving with the famous 10th Submarine Flotilla. In July 1943 she acted as a navigational beacon for American assault convoys on their way to Sicily as part of Operation 'Husky'. She is seen here commanded by Commander Ben Bryant DSO** DSC RN flying the 'Jolly Roger' marked with her 'kills', returning to her depot ship at the end of a war patrol. She survived the war but foundered while being towed to the breaker's yard on 7 January 1946. (*Ken Kelly Collection*)

HM Submarine STRONGBOW in January 1944 shortly after her completion by Scotts of Greenock. The moored flying boats in the background are American-supplied Martin Mariner GR 1s, only 27 of which were supplied to RAF Coastal Command from August 1943. The Command found the type unsuitable and they were withdrawn from service in December and moored in Wig Bay near Stranraer where this photograph must have been taken. STRONGBOW survived the war but was withdrawn from service soon afterwards and broken up at Preston in April 1946.　　　　　　　　　　　　　　　　(*Syd Goodman Collection*)

HM Submarine SURF in the Clyde in March 1943. She was built by Cammell Laird and launched on 10 December 1942. The wartime censor has been kind and the radar and electronic warfare aerials have not been painted out, showing the outfit as completed. The later groups of the 'S' class built under wartime 'emergency' estimates incorporated several improvements such as the 'bandstand' for a single 20mm Oerlikon gun on the after part of the conning-tower. SURF served in the Mediterranean where she sank a German auxiliary and the enemy merchant ship SONIA before deploying to the Indian Ocean where she laid mines in the Malacca Strait and sank a Japanese tug and its barge with gunfire. She was withdrawn from service soon after the end of hostilities and broken up at Faslane from 28 October 1949.   (*Syd Goodman Collection*)

HM Submarine SENESCHAL was built by Scotts of Greenock and, although she was laid down in September 1943, she was not completed until 6 September 1945, four days after the end of the war. She saw operational service for several years after 1945 and is seen here fitted with a snort mast in the lowered position and her deck gun removed to improve underwater performance on 25 March 1952 in the Holy Loch off the Clyde. She was hit by the Danish frigate THETIS off the Isle of Wight on 4 June 1952 during exercises, suffering damage to her masts and periscopes. She was broken up by Clayton and Davie at their Dunston yard from 23 August 1960.

(*Syd Goodman Collection*)

To date this 'S' class submarine is the only British warship to have been given the name STOIC. She was built by Cammell Laird as one of the numerically large second group and completed in 1943. Note the external torpedo tube in the after casing and the Liberty-Ship in the background. Most of her wartime service was in the Far East where she sank a number of Japanese vessels including six small sailing vessels, the coaster KAINAN MARU, a landing craft, the fishing-vessel NANYO MARU No55, the gunboat SHOEI MARU and an un-named coaster. By late 1944 the blockade of Japan was so effective that the Japanese were forced to use small sailing vessels and coasters to move cargoes. She also used her deck gun to bombard warehouses and fuel tanks at Janka Island. She was broken up at Dalmuir in July 1950.

*(Syd Goodman Collection)*

Another boat with a unique name, SHALIMAR was built by Chatham Dockyard as one of the second group of the 'S' class and completed in 1943. She spent most of her service life in the Far East and served with the 2nd Submarine Flotilla in the East Indies Fleet. She bombarded Malacca on 2 November 1944 and sank a total of fourteen Japanese sailing vessels, the minesweeper CHOUN MARU No7, two tugs, three barges, a coaster and damaged five Japanese landing craft. Some of her successes were achieved operating as part of a 'wolf-pack' with SEA DOG. After returning to the UK she was sold for scrap at Troon in July 1950. *(Syd Goodman Collection)*

Built by Scotts but completed by Vickers at Barrow, SEA ROVER was one of the second group of 'S' class submarines completed in 1943. Like many other boats of her class, she had a new name that has not been allocated to any other British warship. She saw service in the Atlantic and in the Eastern Fleet where she sank the Japanese MATSU MARU with gunfire in the Malacca Strait on 3 March 1944. She also torpedoed and sank the transport SHOBU MARU in the Malacca Strait and the auxiliary gunboat KOSHU MARU in the entrance to Penang harbour and numerous, smaller Japanese vessels by gunfire or by boarding them and setting scuttling charges. She saw little post-war service; was sold in October 1949 and broken up at Faslane from June 1950.

*(Syd Goodman Collection)*

HM Submarine P511 was never allocated a name by the Royal Navy. She was originally R-3 of the US Navy, a small coastal boat launched in January 1919 and commissioned at Boston a few months later with the pennant number SS-80. She was de-commissioned by the USN in 1934 but re-commissioned as the Service expanded in August 1940. On 4 November 1941 she was transferred to the RN for use as a training boat until December 1944 when she was deemed to be worn out and unfit for further service. The USN had no use for her and left her in the UK to be scrapped at Troon in 1948.

*(Syd Goodman Collection)*

When Lieutenant Commander 'Freddie' Sherwood DSC RCNVR assumed command of SPITEFUL he was, by a few weeks, the first volunteer reserve officer to be given submarine command in World War 2. After carrying out a war patrol in the Atlantic from December 1943, SPITEFUL joined the 8th Submarine Squadron in the Far East initially based in Ceylon then Fremantle Western Australia as part of the British Pacific Fleet with her depot ship HMS MAIDSTONE. In three patrols she spent 34, 38 and 37 days at sea respectively, a record for an 'S' boat. She sank numerous small Japanese craft and used her deck gun to bombard oil tanks on Christmas Island in the Indian Ocean. She returned to the UK in April 1945 and was lent to the French Navy, renamed SIRENE, between 1952 and 1958. She saw no further use after her return and was broken up at Faslane in 1963.

*(Syd Goodman Collection)*

Another 'S' boat with a unique name, SPARK was built by Scotts and completed in 1944. She saw service with the 8th Submarine Flotilla in the British Pacific Fleet after a single war patrol in the Atlantic and in July 1945 towed XE-1 from Brunei Bay to the Johore Strait north of Singapore, in company with STYGIAN which towed XE-3, to attack Japanese cruisers known to be moored in the Strait. XE-1 was briefed to attack MYOKO and XE-3 to attack TAKAO but XE-1 was delayed and in the event both 'X' craft laid their charges under TAKAO which sank but with its upper-works remaining above the surface. All four boats returned safely from the mission. SPARK saw little service after the war and was broken up at Faslane in 1950.

*(Syd Goodman Collection)*

HM Submarine SPEARHEAD was built by Cammell Laird as another of the 'S' class second group with a unique name and completed on 21 December 1944. She was awarded the Battle Honour Atlantic 1945 and served briefly with the 8th Submarine Flotilla in the British Pacific Fleet but saw no post-war service with the Royal Navy. In 1948 she was sold to the Portuguese Navy and renamed NEPTUNO. SPUR and SAGA were sold at the same time and renamed NARVAL and NAUTILO. NEPTUNO was discarded in 1967.

(*Syd Goodman Collection*)

HM Submarine SIDON was built by Cammell Laird and commissioned on 23 November 1944. She is seen here on 10 September 1952 with her deck gun removed and a lowered snort mast fitted aft of the conning-tower. During 1955 she carried out trial firings of the Mark 12 'Fancy' torpedo, propelled by burning oil fuel and High Test Peroxide. On the morning of 16 June 1955 she had two in her bow tubes while secured alongside her depot ship HMS MAIDSTONE in Portland Harbour when, at 0825, one of them exploded. The warhead did not detonate but the propellant explosion killed 12 men outright, wounded 7 more and damaged water-tight bulkheads, causing the boat to sink, bows first. Her commanding officer, Lieutenant Commander Verry RN ordered the boat to be cleared while a rescue party from MAIDSTONE evacuated the wounded. Among them was temporary Surgeon Lieutenant Charles Eric Rhodes RN who got several men out but suffocated in the toxic gas given off by the explosion on re-entering the boat to look for more. SIDON sank at 0850. Rhodes was posthumously awarded the Albert Medal for his bravery and the boat was raised after a week to recover the 13 bodies which were buried with full naval honours in Portland RN Cemetery. She was subsequently sunk as a sonar target off Portland.

*(Syd Goodman Collection)*

HM Submarine TORBAY, seen here in Plymouth Sound, was first commissioned on 14 January 1941 and earned fame during a series of aggressive war patrols in the Aegean and Eastern Mediterranean commanded by Lieutenant Commander A C C Miers VC DSO* RN in 1941 and 1942. In the most notable of these, Miers guided TORBAY into Corfu Roadstead and spent 17 hours in closely-patrolled enemy waters sinking 2 important stores ships. He was counter-attacked with over 40 depth charges but escaped intact. TORBAY went on to serve in the East Indies Fleet in 1945 but was not retained after the end of hostilities. She was scrapped at Briton Ferry from December 1945. (*Syd Goodman Collection*)

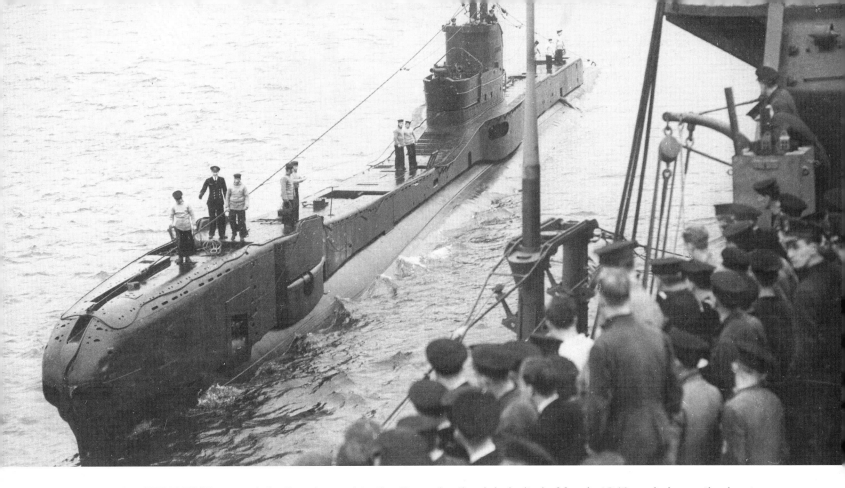

This photograph of TRIDENT was originally released to the Press by the Admiralty in March 1942 and shows the boat returning from the successful patrol in which she torpedoed and damaged the German cruiser PRINZ EUGEN off Norway. In August 1941 TRIDENT's ship's company was presented with a reindeer by the Russian Navy at Polyarnoe as a gesture of Allied solidarity. Once extricated from the boat on its return to the UK, the animal was donated to a zoo but, unfortunately, history does not relate what it had been fed whilst on board. After serving in Home, Mediterranean and Far Eastern waters and sinking a Japanese landing craft off Batu Island in the Dutch East Indies in 1945, she was broken up at Newport in 1946.

*(Steve Bush Collection)*

HM Submarine THUNDERBOLT, seen here in 1942, had a chequered and unusual background as one of the few warships to sink twice with the loss of most of the first and all of the second ship's company. She was built by Cammell Laird as THETIS, one of the first batch of 'T' class boats and sank in Liverpool Bay when an inner torpedo-tube door was opened while the outer was also open allowing an uncontrollable inrush of water. There were 4 survivors but 99 men were lost. She was raised, repaired and re-named THUNDERBOLT in 1940, serving with success in the Atlantic and Mediterranean. One of her more notable actions was to carry frogmen and their 'chariot' underwater vehicles to Palermo harbour where they attached limpet mines to the Italian cruiser ULPIO TRAIANO and the freighter VIMINALE, sinking both. She was lost with all hands due to enemy action off Sicily on 13 March 1943.

(*Steve Bush Collection*)

A 'T' class boat with its vents open in the act of diving. Fourteen were ordered before the war and two further 'emergency' batches ordered during the war. Some of the last batch were cancelled but, in all, some 50 boats were completed. They had a submerged displacement of 1,571 tons, a length of 273 feet 6 inches and diesel engines delivering 2,400 hp on two shafts; electric motors delivered 1,450 hp. Speed on the surface was 15 knots with 9 knots dived. Armament comprised 6 bow tubes with 12 torpedoes and 5 external tubes in the casing which could not be re-loaded on patrol; 2 forward and 3 aft. Most had a single 4-inch gun on the casing forward. (*Syd Goodman Collection*)

HM Submarine TANTALUS on 30 April on 30 April 1943. The three aft-facing external tubes are clearly evident in this aerial view. She served with the 8th Submarine Flotilla in the East Indies Fleet and on 26 February 1945 returned to her depot ship HMS MAIDSTONE in Fremantle, Western Australia, after a war patrol lasting 55 days, the longest carried out by any British submarine in World War II. Whilst on patrol she transited the Lombok Strait to operate in the South China Sea and carried out Air-Sea Rescue duties for the British carrier-borne air attacks on the Palembang refineries. Unfortunately she was not informed of the delay to the second strike and was not there when a pilot ditched at the ASR rendezvous position. When alerted she searched for him for many hours and even used flares at night but found no trace.

(*Syd Goodman Collection*)

HM Submarine TRITON, built at Vickers at Barrow-in-Furness was the first of the 'T' class to be completed in 1937. On 10 September 1939 she torpedoed and sank HMS Oxley in a 'friendly-fire' incident in the North Sea when the latter failed to respond to a recognition challenge. Four days later STURGEON was attacked and was narrowly missed by her sister-ship SWORDFISH in a similar incident. TRITON herself was lost on 18 December 1940 when she was sunk by the Italian torpedo-boat CLIO in the southern Adriatic; the last of a total of twenty-three British submarines sunk by the enemy in 1940.

*(Syd Goodman Collection)*

HM Submarine THISTLE had one of the shortest RN submarine careers. She was built by Vickers at Barrow-in-Furness and launched on 25 October 1939. When the Germans invaded Norway on 9 April 1940 she was ordered to patrol off Stavanger; hours later she was ordered to enter the harbour to attack shipping at the commanding officer's discretion. She had already fired a salvo of torpedoes at a U-boat off Skudenshavn but had not observed the result. She was not heard from again and her fate remained a mystery until after the war when it was learned that the boat she had attacked and missed, U-4, had subsequently stalked THISTLE until 0213 on 10 April when she caught the British boat off guard, torpedoed and sank her. She had the dubious distinction of being the first Allied submarine to be sunk by a U-boat in World War 2.

*(Maritime Photo Library)*

Built by Cammell Laird and launched in November 1940, THRASHER achieved fame in the Mediterranean after attacking a ship off Souda Bay in Crete on 16 February 1942. She was then attacked herself by aircraft and when she surfaced that night to re-charge her batteries, two unexploded bombs were found to be lodged in her casing. Lieutenant P S W Roberts and Petty Officer T W Gould volunteered to crawl into the casing, prize them free and jettison them, knowing that either or both could still explode and that if the boat was attacked the commanding officer would have no choice but to dive, trapping them in the casing where they would drown. They succeeded and both were awarded the Victoria Cross for their actions. In June 1942 she sank the Italian fast sloop DIANA which was carrying technical experts and Axis staff officers to North Africa about a hundred miles north west of Tobruk. After the war she was sold for scrap and broken up at Briton Ferry from March 1947.

*(T.Ferrers-Walker Collection)*

HM Submarine TERRAPIN was built by Vickers and is seen here at Barrow-in-Furness on 19 January 1944, three days before she was first commissioned. One of the third batch of 'T's, she spent most of her wartime service in the Far East and carried out several successful patrols. On 19 May 1945 she was damaged by depth charges from Japanese escort vessels but managed to return to her base at Fremantle. After survey, she was deemed to be beyond economical repair and she returned to the UK only to be scrapped at Troon from April 1946.

*(T. Ferrers-Walker Collection)*

HM Submarine TRESPASSER was one of a number of 'T' boats that were kept in service after 1945. She is seen here on 11 June 1953 after modification with a snort mast but otherwise much as built by Vickers and first commissioned on 25 September 1942. During her war service she sank an Italian patrol vessel and damaged a Japanese gunboat.

(*Syd Goodman Collection*)

HM Submarine TELEMACHUS was another Vickers-built 'T' boat and was launched in June 1943. She continued in service after 1945 and in 1949 deployed to join the 4th Submarine Squadron in Sydney to provide anti-submarine training for the Royal Australian and New Zealand Navies which had no submarine branches of their own. She is seen here at Aden in November 1959 on her way back to the UK from Australia. Apart from the snort mast fitted aft of the conning-tower she is still much as she was when built. At the time she had a complement of 5 officers and 57 men and had 'steamed' 276, 742 miles since first commissioning! She saw no further active service after her return and was scrapped at Charlestown from 25 August 1961.

(*Ken Kelly Collection*)

Another of the submarines that served with the 4th Squadron based in Sydney was THOROUGH seen here in December 1957 after her return to Fort Blockhouse in Gosport with the wooden training ship FOUDROYANT and Portsmouth Dockyard in the background. She travelled home from Australia across the Pacific through the Panama Canal, a distance of some 12,500 miles during which she became the first RN submarine to visit Tahiti. Her commanding officer, Lieutenant Commander Richard Mason RN claimed that after leaving Fort Blockhouse in October 1949 his boat had taken 2,791 days to circumnavigate the world and return.

(*Syd Goodman Collection*)

The 'U' class were originally intended as unarmed training boats and the first 3 were ordered as such in 1936. Whilst under construction they and their successors were modified to have an operational capability with 4 internal and 2 external 21-inch bow torpedo tubes. Eventually 71 of this and the similar 'V' class were built under emergency war programmes. They had a submerged displacement of 740 tons and Paxman diesel engines driving two shafts at 615 hp. This gave a surface speed of only 11 knots but electric motors of 825 hp gave a respectable speed of 10 knots dived. This is HMS UPROAR returning from a patrol on 29 February 1944; she was built by Vickers, launched in November 1940 and adopted by Cirencester in War Week 1941. She was broken up at Inverkeithing from February 1946.

(*Steve Bush Collection*)

HM Submarine UPSTART formed part of the second batch of the 'U' class; she was built by Vickers and launched on 24 November 1942. In 1945 she was lent to the Royal Hellenic Navy and renamed XIPHIAS; her sister-boat UNTIRING was also lent and renamed AMFITRITI. Both were returned to the Royal Navy in 1952 and refitted for further service as submarine targets from 1953 onwards with their original names. UPSTART was deleted from the active list in 1956 and on 31 July 1957 she was towed from Portsmouth and sunk south of the Needles, Isle of WIght, for use as a bottom target.

(*Syd Goodman Collection*)

HM Submarines UNITED and UPRIGHT seen secured together on their return to the UK from the Mediterranean where both had served with distinction. Both were built by Vickers at Barrow-in-Furness. UNITED was launched in December 1941 and after arriving in the Mediterranean sank the Italian destroyer BOMBARDIERE off western Sicily on 17 January 1943; the Italian armed merchant cruiser OLBIA off Cape Spartivento on 20 June 1943 and the Italian submarine SAN REMO in the Gulf of Taranto on 15 July 1943. UPRIGHT was launched in April 1940 and sank the Italian cruiser ARMANDO DIAZ east of Sfax in Tunisia on 25 February 1941. On 28 May 1941 she put a landing party ashore near Punto Stilo Light in Southern Italy that blew up a railway line and in September she sank the Italian torpedo-boat ALBATROSS. She shared in sinking two transports off Tripoli with UNBEATEN, UPHOLDER and URSULA. UNITED and UPRIGHT were both withdrawn from service at the end of the war and broken up at Troon in 1946.

(*Syd Goodman Collection*)

HM Submarine VISIGOTH was built by Vickers at Barrow-in-Furness, launched in November 1943 and completed on 9 April 1944 as a unit of the 'V' class, essentially an improved version of the 'U' class. They were partially welded and had a greater diving depth. Twenty boats of this class were cancelled when the war in Europe ended. VISIGOTH saw service in the Mediterranean and on 24 September 1944 she attacked small enemy sailing vessels, used as transports, with gunfire in Strali Harbour in Crete. She was withdrawn from service after the war, sold to T W Ward in March 1949 and broken up for scrap at Hayle in Cornwall from April 1950.

*(Syd Goodman Collection)*

HM Submarine VENGEFUL was built by Vickers as a unit of the 'V' class; effectively a repeat 'U' but with a number of significant improvements including thicker hull plating. She was launched on 20 July 1944 and is seen here on 14 October 1944 shortly after completion. She saw no operational service with the Royal Navy and was one of 4 'V's transferred to the Royal Hellenic Navy immediately after completion. She was renamed DELFIN and served with the Greek Fleet until 1957 when she was returned to the Royal Navy. There was no operational requirement for her and she was broken up at Gateshead.

(*T. Ferrers-Walker Collection*)

The 'X' class were a series of midget submarines built to attack enemy warships in harbour. They had to be towed to the attack area by 'S' or 'T' boats but had a small diesel engine, actually a modified London bus engine, of 45 hp that gave a surface speed of 6 knots and a 30 hp electric motor that gave an underwater speed of 5 knots for short periods. Their primary weapons were 4,000lb high-explosive charges which were released under the target. This is an improved version X 52, one of 4 built by Vickers in 1954, given the appropriate name SHRIMP. They were used for training and retained for their potential war capability until 1961 when they were deleted from the active list. SHRIMP was broken up in 1965.

(*National Museum of the Royal Navy*)

One of four improved 'X' class boats built by Vickers, the appropriately named STICKLEBACK was launched in 1954 and used by the RN for training although she had the latent ability to attack Soviet harbours if the Cold War turned hot. Following the reduction in the size of the RN after the 1957 Defence Review she was sold to Sweden in July 1958 and renamed SPIGGEN, the Swedish translation of STICKLEBACK. She was used to train harbour defences against midget submarine attack until 1977 when she was returned to the UK. She is now on display at the Imperial War Museum, Duxford.

(*Syd Goodman Collection*)

The 'A' class were ordered from 1943 onwards and intended for operations against the Japanese in the Pacific. They were essentially enlarged and improved 'T's but with an all-welded hull assembled from pre-fabricated sections which reduced the build-time from the 'T's average of 15 months to about 8. Even so, none were operational before the end of hostilities. This is ALCIDE in her original configuration off Cawsand Bay in Plymouth Sound during 1947. Note the twin 20mm Oerlikon gun mounting on the 'bandstand' aft of the bridge.

*(Syd Goodman Collection)*

HM Submarine AUROCHS was built by Vickers and launched in July 1945. She left the UK in January 1956 and joined the 4th Submarine Squadron in Sydney where she was used to train the Royal Australian and New Zealand Navies in anti-submarine warfare. Her return passage to the UK was made across the Pacific making her the second British submarine to circumnavigate the world when she arrived back at Gosport on December 1958. She was surveyed in 1964 and found to be in poor condition, not worth refitting, and subsequently scrapped at Troon in 1967. Forty-six 'A' class boats were originally ordered but only 18 were launched; the rest being scrapped when the war ended unexpectedly early. Sixteen of those launched were commissioned and 2, ACE and ACHATES, were used for crush-depth testing and expended in 1950.

*(Syd Goodman Collection)*

U-570 was a Type VIIC U-boat built by Blohm and Voss at Hamburg and completed in May 1941. Only four days into her first operational patrol on 27 August 1941 she was attacked off Iceland by an RAF Hudson which damaged her with depth charges after which she was captured by the anti-submarine trawler NORTHERN CHIEF, supported by the destroyers BURWELL and NIAGARA. She was subsequently commissioned into the RN as HMS GRAPH on 19 September 1941 and used initially for a series of trials and evaluations, one of which revealed her safe diving depth of 750 feet, much deeper than contemporary RN boats and below the maximum setting on depth charges at the time. Later she was used as an operational boat until defects and the lack of spare parts led to her being reduced to reserve in February 1944. A month later she ran aground on the west coast of Islay while being towed to a Clyde scrap yard. She was partially broken up in situ in 1947 but her remains were, until recently, still visible at low tide. (*T. Ferrers-Walker Collection*)

After the German surrender in 1945 seventeen U-boats were allocated to the RN, some of which were commissioned temporarily for trials. One of these was U-1407, a Type XXI boat fitted with turbine machinery for which energy was supplied by burning diesel oil in decomposed hydrogen peroxide (HTP). This gave her an impressive maximum underwater speed of 25 knots although she had conventional diesels and a motor for use when high speed was not required. She was refitted by Vickers at Barrow-in-Furness and Professor Walter, who designed the machinery, was brought to Barrow to supervise the work. The boat was commissioned as METEORITE and carried out extensive trials of HTP propulsion which led to the design and construction of the two 'Ex' class experimental boats which became, for a time, the fastest submarines in the world. She was re-fitted with a more streamlined conning tower in 1948 but was eventually sold to T W Ward at Barrow in September 1949 for scrap when the trials were completed.

*(Syd Goodman Collection)*

HM Submarine ARTFUL photographed on 16 October 1952. She has undergone some modification work and is seen here with all the guns removed to reduce underwater drag. The 'A's had a submerged displacement of 1,620 tons, diesel engines of 4,300 hp and electric motors of 1,250 hp. Speed on the surface was 18 knots and underwater 8 knots. They had ten torpedo tubes for 26 torpedoes or mines.

(*Syd Goodman Collection*)

HM Submarines ALDERNEY and ALARIC at Gibraltar in July 1950 with the depot ship FORTH and other submarines in the background. Two of the forward torpedo tubes were outside the pressure hull and their bow caps can be seen open. The high, flared bow shape was intended to allow fast surface transit speeds on passage to patrol areas in the Pacific. The clean, welded construction lines are also evident.

*(Ken Kelly Collection)*

There were reports in 1944 that the Germans had developed submarines with high underwater speed and the Admiralty responded by modifying SERAPH as a high-speed target-boat to help develop new anti-submarine tactics. Drastic streamlining and propellers of greater pitch gave an underwater speed of 12 knots. Postwar analysis of German developments led the Admiralty to streamline 5 further 'S' boats one of which, SLEUTH, is seen here on 13 March 1947. Note the rounded conning-tower and the removal of all extraneous equipment from the casing to reduce drag. She was broken up in 1958.

(*Syd Goodman Collection*)

HM Submarine SCOTSMAN was rebuilt as a 'super-Seraph' with electric motors of 3,600 hp instead of the original 1,300. Hull volume was limited, however, and smaller diesels of only 307 hp had to be substituted for the originals. She achieved an underwater speed of 16.33 knots on trials but could only re-charge her batteries slowly so high-speed bursts had to be followed by lengthy periods re-charging. She was sunk deliberately off Kames Bay in Bute and then raised in June 1964 to practice salvage skills and equipment before being broken up.

*(Syd Goodman Collection)*

HM Submarine SCOTSMAN was used for a number of streamlining experiments after her modernisation which were intended to investigate potential improvements in hydrodynamic efficiency that could improve her maximum underwater speed still further. These included the complete removal of the bridge fin at one stage and the fitting of a range of experimental propellers. She is seen here with radically modified casing structures intended to optimise water flow over the hull at high underwater speeds but which must have made the movement of berthing parties somewhat difficult when coming alongside.

*(Syd Goodman Collection)*

HM Submarine SELENE, one of the early 'S' conversions in Plymouth Sound during 1953. She was built by Cammell Laird and launched on 24 April 1944. After streamlining she was used for trials and training before being broken up at Gateshead in 1961.

(*Syd Goodman Collection*)

A number of 'T' boats were converted after the war to achieve high underwater speed. In the first group external torpedo tubes and guns were removed and a streamlined 'fin'-type conning tower replaced the original. They were cut in half amidships and a new section twelve feet long inserted which contained two more electric motors and a fourth section of batteries. Underwater speed was doubled. This is one of the group, THERMOPYLAE, on 11 November 1952, shortly after conversion. Note the clean lines of the 'fin' and sonar dome forward. (*Syd Goodman Collection*)

Another of the first group of 'T's to be modified was TACITURN; she had a new section fourteen feet long inserted but was otherwise similar to her modified sisters. A number of wartime boats were upgraded to keep the British submarine force viable as the Cold War developed as there were delays in the design and construction of new boats. Submarines were no longer intended for use against surface ships but instead targeted the growing and already large Soviet submarine fleet.

*(Syd Goodman Collection)*

HM Submarine TRUNCHEON was one of the second batch of 'T' conversions. These boats had welded hulls which allowed more extensive changes to be worked into them including new sections twenty feet long containing motors and extra batteries. She is seen here on 8 January 1963 in what was by then the standard black paint scheme for Royal Navy submarines with white pennant numbers painted on the 'fin'. In January 1968 she was sold to the Israeli Navy to replace DAKAR, formerly TOTEM, which had been lost at sea. She was renamed DOLPHIN. *(Syd Goodman Collection)*

Built by Vickers at Barrow-in-Furness and launched 25 June 1945 by Mrs Molly Wallis, wife of Doctor Barnes Wallis, ALDER-NEY was the second 'A' class boat to be streamlined and spent part of her life in the 6th Submarine Squadron based at Halifax, Nova Scotia training the Royal Canadian Navy in anti-submarine operations. She arrived at Cairn Ryan in Scotland to be broken up for scrap by Shipbreaking (Queenborough) in August 1972.

*(Syd Goodman Collection)*

The most modern of the British war-built submarines the 'A' class were improved and streamlined between 1955 and 1960 to suit them for their new anti-submarine role. They received higher-capacity batteries and new bows, sterns and 'fin' conning-towers. Larger electric motors were not fitted, however, and so underwater speed was not increased greatly. AMBUSH is seen here, inboard, at Aden in November 1959 on her way to join the Far East Fleet. The boat outboard is the un-modernised TELEMACHUS on her way back, west-bound, to the UK from Australia. *(Ken Kelly Collection)*

Built by Cammell laird at Birkenhead and launched on 30 May 1957, GRAMPUS was the third 'Porpoise' class boat into the water. In 1968 she spent three weeks under the polar ice-cap looking for holes through which submarines could surface and received superficial damage in the process. On 11 January 1968 she was caught in the nets of the French trawler FOMA-LHOUT in the English Channel. Luckily neither vessel was damaged and she was able to surface and clear the nets, a task which took three hours. In 1972 she took part in a joint UK/US oceanographic trial in the Atlantic with USS TIGRONE. From 1976 she was used as a harbour training boat at Gosport and in 1979 she was placed on the Disposals List but in February 1980 she was removed from the List and converted into a static target in Portsmouth Dockyard. She was sunk as a seabed sonar target later in 1980.

*(Syd Goodman Collection)*

The 'Porpoise' class were the first submarines to be designed and built for the Royal Navy after World War II. Six were ordered in 1951 and 2 more in 1954. Improved design methods and the use of special UXW steel allowed a diving depth of 500 feet and torpedoes could be fired at much greater depth than in any previous British boat. Top speed underwater was 16 knots and they had an endurance of 9,000 miles. This is NARWHAL in 1959 not long after her completion; she was built by Vickers and launched on 25 October 1957. After a successful career she was sunk off Portland in June 1980 and raised three weeks later by the Swedish salvage ship HEBE III and 2 RMAS vessels as part of a salvage exercise before being broken up.

*(Syd Goodman Collection)*

HM Submarine SEALION was built by Cammell Laird and launched on 31 December 1959 as the last of the 'Porpoises'. The class had a submerged displacement of 2,405 tons with six bow and two stern torpedo tubes. Eight torpedoes were carried in the tubes with 22 reloads. They were intended to spend most of their time on patrol dived, using the snort to run diesels and re-charge the batteries. The diesels generated 3,680 hp and the electric motors 6,000 hp. She has three masts raised, UHF radio aerial, radar and the search periscope.

(*Syd Goodman Collection*)

HM Submarine EXCALIBUR was one of two unarmed, experimental submarines built to evaluate turbine machinery powered by burning diesel oil in decomposed High Test Peroxide (HTP). All the HTP equipment was grouped at the fore-end of the unmanned engine room and the HTP itself was stowed in PVC bags fitted in free-flooding tanks outside the pressure hull. They had a maximum underwater speed of 27 knots which could be sustained for three hours. She was built by Vickers, launched on 25 February 1955 and for a while she and her sister EXPLORER were the fastest submarines in the world. They were also used to investigate the control of high-speed submarines and, latterly, as high-speed submarine targets. EXCALIBUR was discarded in 1965 and broken up in 1970.

*(Ben Warlow Collection)*

The 'Oberon' class was a repeat of the 'Porpoise' design but with a number of significant improvements. QT28 steel replaced UXW to give an even greater diving depth and the 'O' boats proved to be the quietest of their generation. Thirteen were built for the Royal Navy and others were exported to Australia, Canada, Brazil and Chile. This is OTTER, built by Scotts and completed in August 1962.

(*Syd Goodman Collection*)

During March 1965 the British submarines OPOSSUM, seen here, and FINWHALE took part in the NATO exercise 'Portent' during which they surfaced near the fringe of the Arctic pack ice at 76 degrees North. Her commanding officer Lieutenant Commander W L Owen RN is seen with members of his ship's company on the ice alongside their boat. (*Syd Goodman Collection*)

A nostalgic photograph of boats alongside the original home of the Submarine Branch, HMS DOLPHIN at Fort Blockhouse in Gosport. It is now (2011) the site of the RN Submarine Museum and many of the buildings survive but DOLPHIN itself closed in 1999.

(*Syd Goodman Collection*)

The 'O' boats had long and successful careers in the Royal Navy, becoming familiar sights to the public when not on patrol. This is OLYMPUS passing under Tower Bridge during a visit to London. She was built by Vickers and completed in 1962. In that year the white pennant numbers were removed from the 'fins' of British boats so that they could not be identified if they were involved in a close-quarter situation with their Soviet counterparts.    (*Syd Goodman Collection*)

A Sea King HAS 2 helicopter of 819 Naval Air Squadron from RNAS PRESTWICK winching a crew-member off ORACLE's 'fin'. Winching required a high level of skill from the pilot since he could not see the 'fin' below and behind him. The hover was established with reference to the bow, making fine adjustments following the instructions called by the winch-operator at the door.

*(Crown Copyright/MoD)*

HM Submarine OSIRIS inboard with OTTER outboard alongside the Clyde Submarine Base, HMS NEPTUNE, at Faslane. The fibre-glass 'huts' covered the fore-hatch which was kept open in harbour in order to keep rain out and warmth in. OSIRIS has her UHF aerial and electronic warfare masts raised. (*Crown Copyright/MoD*)

The name DREADNOUGHT was selected for the first British nuclear-powered submarine which was ordered in 1957. To hasten her entry into service, the Prime Minister and US President agreed in 1958 that she should be completed with an American S5W nuclear power plant. Thus she had an after end identical to USS SKIPJACK and a fore-end designed around British studies and conformal sonar array. The 'fin' was further aft than in American boats and the forward hydroplanes were placed near the bow, not on the 'fin' to give better low-speed control. She had a greater dived speed than any previous British submarine and a much greater diving depth. She was de-commissioned in 1983 after twenty years in service and has been laid up at Rosyth ever since. No British nuclear-powered submarine has yet been broken up. (*Syd Goodman Collection*)

The 'Valiant' class nuclear-powered submarines which followed DREADNOUGHT substituted a British nuclear plant for the American S5W. VALIANT was ordered in August 1960 followed by WARSPITE nine months later. The latter was built by Vickers, completed in 1967 and is seen here at the US Navy pier at Port Canaveral in 1984. In 1990 VALIANT and WARSPITE were found to have cracks in their primary circuits and, although these were repairable, their remaining short life under the defence run-down at the time made the work uneconomical and it was not carried out. Like all other British nuclear-powered boats, they have been laid up since their withdrawal from service. (*US Navy*)

HM Submarine WARSPITE leaving San Carlos Water in the Falkland Islands to carry out a patrol in the South Atlantic. Nuclear-powered hunter/killer submarines have the ability to cross vast distances unseen and then to dominate large areas of ocean. Sometimes they reveal their presence, as here, to show potential aggressors that, beyond doubt, British possessions are defended.

*(Crown Copyright/MoD)*

Three 'later Valiants' were ordered after the gap caused by the Polaris-boats' construction. This is COURAGEOUS, the first British boat to deploy the American Sub-Harpoon anti-shipping missile. These later boats incorporated many detail improvements; their Rolls-Royce pressurised water cooled nuclear reactors powered English Electric steam turbines developing 15,000 hp giving a speed of 22 knots on the surface and 28 knots dived. Their submerged displacement was 4,745 tons. COURAGEOUS was paid off in 1992.

*(Crown Copyright/MoD)*

HM Submarine CONQUEROR 'on the step' at high speed on the surface in July 1978. In 1982 she sank the Argentine cruiser GENERAL BELGRANO with torpedoes during operations to liberate the Falkland Islands, ensuring that no other Argentine warship would enter waters so clearly dominated by British submarines. On her return to the UK, her commanding officer, Commander Christopher Wreford-Brown DSO RN kept alive the Branch tradition by flying a Jolly Roger flag marked with her operational 'kill'. She was the first nuclear-powered submarine to fire in anger and when she was withdrawn from service in 2005 she remained the only SSN to have sunk an enemy ship with torpedoes. *(Crown Copyright/MoD)*

The decision taken by the British Government in February 1963 to replace manned RAF bombers with Polaris ballistic missiles carried in nuclear-powered submarines led to an order for five 'R' class boats, later reduced to four. RESOLUTION, seen here, was built by Vickers and was the first to complete in 1967. British-designed bow and stern sections were mated with an American-designed missile compartment with launch-tubes for 16 Polaris A-3 missiles together with fire-control equipment. Each missile had a range of 2,500 nautical miles and a British nuclear warhead. The powerplant was the same as that in VALIANT but the greater submerged displacement reduced the maximum speed underwater to 25 knots. The missile hatch covers are plainly visible in this overhead view off the Clyde. (*Crown Copyright/MoD*)

HM Submarine REPULSE completed in 1968 and is seen here during April 1971 in Plymouth Sound with the Breakwater in the background. The 'R's were 426 feet long with a submerged displacement of 7,381 tons. For self-defence against other submarines and hostile surface ships they were armed with six bow 21-inch torpedo tubes. The accommodation area forward of the missile compartment had three decks which allowed good domestic facilities for the 147 officers and men.

*(Syd Goodman Collection)*

HM Submarine REVENGE was the last of the British Polaris boats, built by Cammell Laird and completed in 1969. The Government had insisted in 1963 that Polaris must assume the British national deterrent duty from 1969 and the project delivered that capability on time and on cost. The 'R's left an impressive record and when the last boat was withdrawn in 1996 they had carried out an unbroken sequence of 229 patrols during which, fortunately, they were never required to fire a shot in anger.

*(Crown Copyright/MoD)*

The six boats of the 'Swiftsure' class represented a logical step forward from the 'Valiant' design with an improved hull design, more capable sonar and an underwater speed of 30 knots. SUPERB, seen here in the Clyde, was built by Vickers and completed in 1976, shortly before this photograph was taken. Her sister-boat SPLENDID was the first British submarine to be fitted to carry Tomahawk land-attack cruise missiles in 1998. SUPERB was withdrawn from service at Devonport on 28 September 2008.

*(Crown Copyright/MoD)*

HM Submarine SPARTAN entering the Clyde Submarine Base fitted with a container aft of the 'fin' for carrying Special Forces' swimmers to their objective. She was fitted with an improved reactor core between 1987 and 1993 but was withdrawn from service earlier than originally intended in 2006 when the British Government decided to reduce the number of British nuclear-powered submarines in service as a cost-saving measure. Note the MoD Police RHIB between the cameraman and SPARTAN; boats in the Clyde are protected against intervention by protestors or terrorists while they are manoeuvring in restricted waters.

(*Donald Donaldson*)

The seven 'Trafalgars' are numerically the largest class of nuclear-powered submarines built to date for the Royal Navy. They are among the quietest nuclear boats in any Navy. This is TRAFALGAR herself, built by Vickers and completed in 1983. She was capable of carrying Tomahawk land-attack cruise missiles but was withdrawn from service early in 2009 as part of a reduction in the number of Royal Navy submarines.

*(Crown Copyright/MoD)*

The 'Trafalgar' class submarine TURBULENT passing through the narrows into Faslane Naval base. The image clearly shows the acoustic tiles, thousands of which are fixed to the hull and fin to help mask the boat's sonar signature. She is due to be taken out of service in 2011.

(*Nick Newns*)

HM Submarine TURBULENT seen surfacing at the North Pole through the periscope of SUPERB in 1988. The 'Trafalgar' class have a dived displacement of 5,200 tons and a speed of over 30 knots underwater. They have a ship's company of 130 and five torpedo tubes in the bow. Armament includes Spearfish guided-torpedoes and Tomahawk land-attack cruise missiles.

*(Crown Copyright/MoD)*

The 'Upholder' class was the last British conventional submarine design. Originally 19 boats were planned to replace the 'Oberons' and 'Porpoises' but only four were built, one by Vickers and three by Cammell Laird between 1989 and 1993. Defence economies after the end of the Cold War led to all of them being withdrawn and laid up in 1995. This is UPHOLDER herself during her brief period of service. All four were bought by Canada and renamed as the Victoria class, entering service from 2000 after being refitted in the UK. They are exceptionally quiet diesel electric boats with a dived speed of 20 knots and a complement of 48. Since their withdrawal the Royal Navy has only operated nuclear-powered submarines. *(VSEL)*

The British deterrent has been taken over since 1995 by the 4 boats of the 'Vanguard' class, each with a submerged displacement of 15,000 tons and armed with 16 Trident D5 missiles. This is VENGEANCE, the last of the class to join the Fleet, built by Vickers and completed in 1999. She is passing through the narrows after sailing from Faslane and is being protected by Royal Marines in armed RHIBs. Note the ballistic panels fitted along the side of the missile compartment intended to protect against damage from any rocket-propelled grenade attack by terrorists.

*(John Crae)*

The shape of things to come. ASTUTE and her 'A' class sisters will augment the remaining 'T' class boats and eventually replace all the existing nuclear-powered hunter/killer boats in the Royal Navy. She has a highly-developed hull form giving the distinctive shape seen here from starboard and a high, but classified, underwater speed. She has six bow tubes and can carry Tomahawk missiles and torpedoes. She was completed in 2009 by BAE Systems, formerly Vickers, at Barrow-in-Furness.

*(John Newth)*

HM Submarine AMBUSH is the second boat of the 'Astute' class. Ordered at the same time as ASTUTE on 17 March 1997, work did not start on her until October 2003, nearly three years after her sister-boat. She is now afloat, scheduled to commence trials in 2011 and due to enter operational service in 2012. The 'Astutes' are the first class of British submarines not to be fitted with traditional periscopes. Instead they have two CM010 'optronic' masts which are electro-optical, non-hull-penetrating units which carry radio-frequency, infra-red and high-definition colour television sensors. The hull and fin are covered with 39,000 acoustic tiles to reduce the boat's sonar signature.

*(Mike Vallance/BAE Systems)*

# INDEX